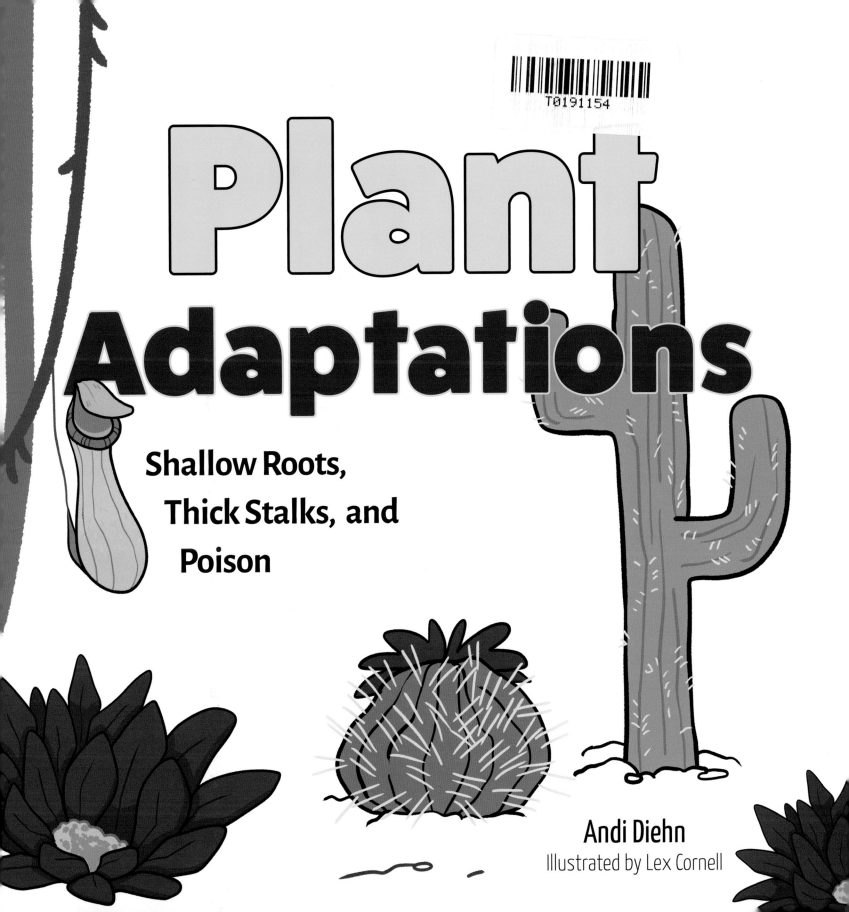

Plant Adaptations

Shallow Roots, Thick Stalks, and Poison

Andi Diehn

Illustrated by Lex Cornell

EXPLORE MORE PICTURE BOOK ADAPTATIONS!

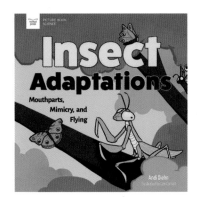

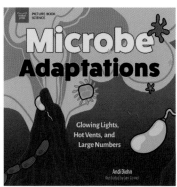

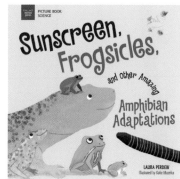

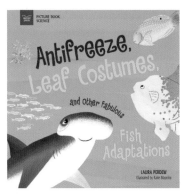

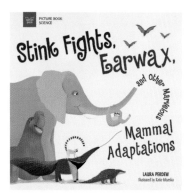

Check out more titles at www.nomadpress.net

Nomad Press

A division of Nomad Communications

10 9 8 7 6 5 4 3 2 1

This book was manufactured by
CGB Printers, North Mankato, Minnesota
November 2024, Job #1082659

ISBN Softcover: 978-1-64741-127-5
ISBN Hardcover: 978-1-64741-124-4

Educational Consultant, Marla Conn

Questions regarding the ordering of this book should be addressed to
Nomad Press
PO Box 1036, Norwich, VT 05055
www.nomadpress.net

Printed in the United States.

Why does a seedling grow up and its roots grow down?
Why do maple leaves change color and turn brown?
Why does a cactus have sharp spiky spines?
Why does a rainforest have lots of vines?

From tiny seed to towering tree,
Plants changed, evolutionarily!
Adapting to environments hot and cold,
To when rain was scarce, when water flowed.

Plants endured, thrived, and stayed alive,
Changing form and behavior so the species survived.
And now we have plants of all shapes and sizes.
What's growing in your garden?
Any surprises?

Do you have plants where you live?

A spider plant in your living room?

A snake plant on the windowsill?

Bushes in the backyard?

All of these plants have **adaptations** that help them survive.

How did the plant say goodbye?

....

"I MUST BE LEAF-ING NOW!"

**Have you ever seen
a saguaro cactus?**

Maybe you've seen a
picture or visited the
Sonoran Desert! That's
where saguaro cactuses
grow—where
the air is hot,
the soil is sandy, and
the sun beats down
almost every day
of the year.

Saguaros have adapted
to that climate.

Their skin has a thick,
waxy coating
that keeps moisture from
escaping. Their roots are
shallow, so rainwater
doesn't have to travel
far to reach them.

And those
sharp bristles keep
other desert creatures
from feeding on them.

Ouch!

Put a saguaro cactus in a rainforest and it probably wouldn't thrive.

But in the desert, it can live for hundreds of years!

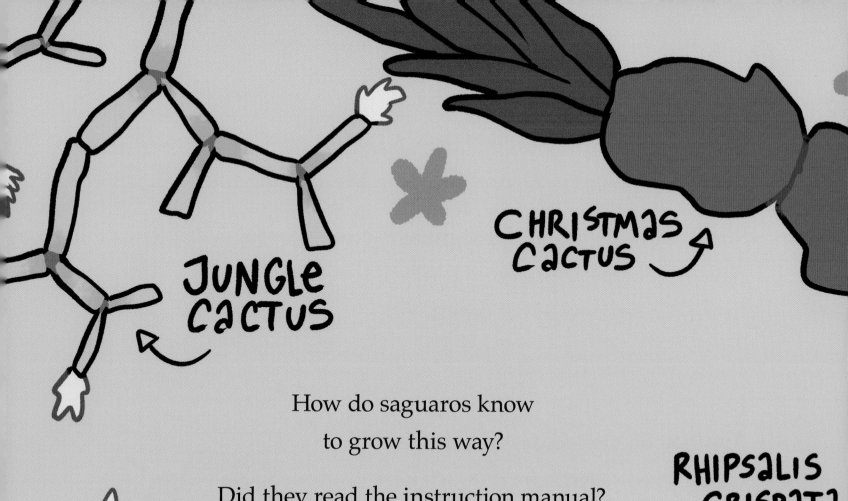

JUNGLE CACTUS

CHRISTMAS CACTUS

RHIPSALIS CRISPATA

How do saguaros know
to grow this way?

Did they read the instruction manual?

Did they look it up at the library?

NO!

**THEY
ADAPTED!**

What is a
snowman's favorite
type of vegetable?

....

A SNOWPEA!

So, what is adaptation?

Adaptation means gaining characteristics to better
survive in an environment. It takes a loooooong time.

Some plants—such as the saguaro cactus—
have developed **traits** that let them live
in the hot dryness of the desert.

Plants with features that
help them survive
live long enough to pass down these
characteristics to their **offspring.**

Because the offspring have the same characteristics as their parents, they are also the ones to survive.

As years pass, the characteristics that don't help with survival appear less often.

Let's look at more examples of adaptation.

We've talked about the saguaro cactus that grows in the desert—how about plants that grow in a much different **climate?**

As you might guess
from the name,

rainforests

get **a lot of**
water!

And while plants need water to survive, too much water can be bad for them.

What kind of bean never grows in a garden?
....
A JELLY BEAN!

8

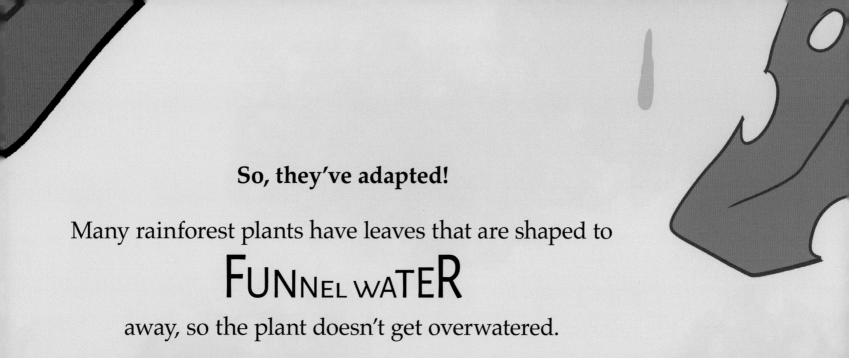

So, they've adapted!

Many rainforest plants have leaves that are shaped to

FUNₙₑₗ waTeR

away, so the plant doesn't get overwatered.

And the leaves often have

a waxy surface

that rain rolls right over.

What about plants that have to survive harsh winters?

Adaptation to the rescue!

Some plants become **dormant** in the winter.
This means they stop growing during the cold months.

They're not dead—it's more like they're
taking a long winter's nap!

Maple trees have a
very sweet adaptation.

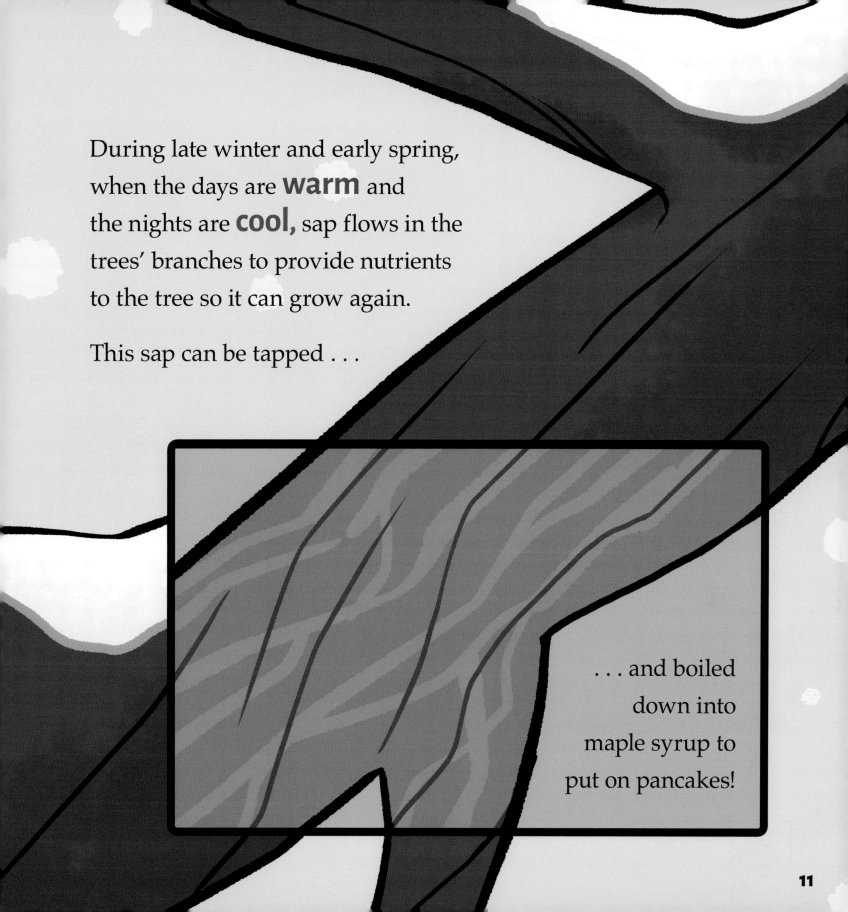

During late winter and early spring, when the days are **warm** and the nights are **cool,** sap flows in the trees' branches to provide nutrients to the tree so it can grow again.

This sap can be tapped . . .

. . . and boiled down into maple syrup to put on pancakes!

Let's look at another adaptation.

Most plants grow in soil and
absorb nutrients through their roots.

But some plants absorb nutrients
through their leaves! They can
grow on other plants or trees.

These plants are called **epiphytes.**

They have adapted to get their
nutrients from the air, dust,
animal waste, and water.

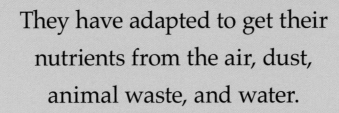

Have you ever eaten pineapple?

Pineapples are epiphytes.

Pineapples and other epiphytes have adapted so they don't need to live in a pot or in the ground.

How else might plants get the **nutrients** they need to live?

Which herb is best
at cheerleading?

ENCOURAGE-MINT!

Have you ever heard of **carnivorous** plants?
These plants eat other living creatures!

Venus flytraps are carnivorous plants
that grow in sandy soil.

Although the plants get some

nutrients from the soil

and air, they need more!

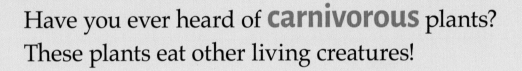

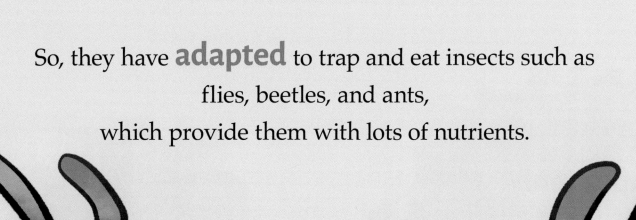

So, they have **adapted** to trap and eat insects such as
flies, beetles, and ants,
which provide them with lots of nutrients.

The trap is made of
two parts that look like
clamshells.

The plant can sense
when an insect
has crawled inside,
and **SNAPS** shut!

Dinner is served!

While carnivorous plants are on the lookout for food, some plants are working hard to keep from being eaten.

Guess what helps?

Adaptation!

Some plants produce **toxins** that can make whatever eats them very sick.

Kidney beans are one of these plants.

The raw beans are poisonous, which
keeps creatures from eating them.

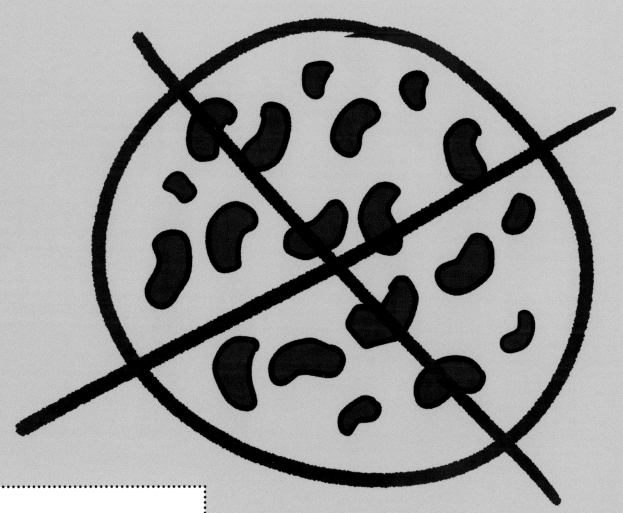

What's a tailor's favorite
kind of vegetable?
....
A STRING BEAN!

So, why do we put beans in our chili?

We've adapted, too.

Early humans discovered fire and put it to good use for cooking food. After we soak and cook kidney beans, they are safe to eat!

Can you think of other food we cook to make safe to eat?

Other plants use poison, too.

Have you ever had a case of poison ivy?

ITCHY!

Plants such as
poison ivy,
poison oak, and
poison sumac
release an oil when their leaves are broken or
crushed that many people are allergic to.

This adaptation means people tend
to leave those plants alone!

Plants want to be left alone, but they
also want to **reproduce.**

Adaptation can help!

Some plants have adaptations to help attract pollinators.

Irises have **nectar guides**

that show bees and
other pollinators
where to go to find pollen.

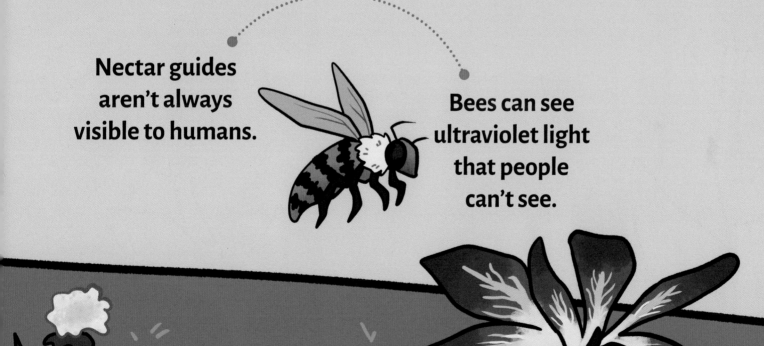

**Nectar guides
aren't always
visible to humans.**

**Bees can see
ultraviolet light
that people
can't see.**

Adaptations are key to survival
for every living creature!

Follow the Sun!

What You Need

fast growing seeds, such as bean seeds - large, sealable bag - damp paper towels - sunny window

What You Do

- Soak the seeds overnight. This will help them sprout sooner.

- Place your damp paper towels in your plastic bag.

- Place a few seeds into the paper towels.

- Tightly seal your plastic bag.

- Tape your bag onto a sunny window.

- During the next few days, your seeds will start to sprout, and your plants will grow!

Think About It!

Which direction does the seedling grow? Which way do the roots grow? What might happen if the plant roots grew toward the sun and the leaves grew under the ground?

Strawberries are the only fruit with seeds on the outside.

Plants can communicate with each other through chemicals they send underground to the areas around them.

Do you like the smell of freshly mown grass? That smell is a distress signal that the grass puts out when it's cut!

Those baby carrots you get from the grocery store aren't babies! They come from big carrots that have been whittled down into bite-size snacks.

Sunflowers follow the sun with their flowerheads as it passes across the sky from east to west.

The Great Basin Bristlecone Pine is believed to be the oldest living tree species! It lives in California and is about 5,000 years old.

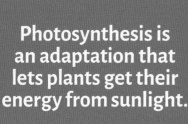

Photosynthesis is an adaptation that lets plants get their energy from sunlight.

Glossary

adaptation: a change that a living thing makes to become better suited to its environment.

carnivorous: a plant or animal that eats meat.

characteristic: a feature or quality.

climate: the weather patterns in an area during a long period of time.

desert: an area that gets very little rain.

dormant: when plants stop growing.

environment: the area in which something lives.

epiphyte: a plant that gets its food and moisture directly from the air and usually lives on another plant.

nutrient: a substance in food, soil, water, or air that living things need to live and grow.

offspring: the young of a plant, insect, or animal.

photosynthesis: how plants turn sunlight and water into food to grow.

pollinator: an insect or other animal that transfers pollen from the male part of a flower to the female part of a flower.

rainforest: a forest in a hot climate that gets a lot of rain every year, so the plants are very green and grow a lot.

reproduce: to produce offspring.

species: a group of plants or animals that are closely related and produce offspring.

toxin: a poisonous or harmful substance.

trait: a characteristic.

ultraviolet: a type of light that humans can't see.